Connecting To Source

Connecting To Source

A Path To Self-Discovery Through Verse

The Mother Love Series

Linda Barry Tuohy

Connecting to Source

Published 2022 by Linda Barry Tuohy

First Edition

ISBN: 978-1-7391296-7-5

Visit the author's website at www.lbt.ie

Illustrations by Parvathi Venkitaraman (www.parvathiv.com)

Design & publishing services provided by JM Agency

www.jm.agency

Dedication

To My Mother, My Daughter, My Husband, My Son
My Brothers, My Father

To all my immediate related Family and those that are as close through Friendships Born

Foreword

Connecting to Source - a path to self-discovery in verse is the first book of poetry that Linda has written. It stems from her journey from entrepreneurial business woman to reconciling the death of her mother and father within a short eighteen month period. Her discovery of the world of meditation and realisation was made in 2010, after the economic crash of what was known as the Celtic Tiger in her home country of Ireland.

Connecting to Source, part of the Mother Love Series, is a collection of her works as she embraces her love of nature through mountains wild, forest streams and oceans of waves. Diving into the world of self-realisation and her quest to discover her inner blockages, Linda connects with her own self-love, something she had closed off early in life.

Connecting to Source gives her unique perspective as a woman, a mother, a daughter, a sister, a wife, and as someone entering her wise woman wisdom years. The collection is a coming together of mind, body and soul in the peace and tranquility of life; a journey of self-realisation through family living in our modern society today.

Contents

Love Within

Come back to the stillness of
the love within.....

Home

I'm gone, a shadow
Has awakened me
Where is the beloved
I do not know the name

One week is all it took
Disappearing calmness
The quiet within
I miss my beloved of being

Burning inside, endless
Mind torture invalids
The noisy sleep,
I am trapped, I cannot
Find my place.

Where is my beloved

Pure Love

Gently she weaves her touch
Lightly on shoulder tense,
I am here Señor, come to be
Come to me, gently gently
the light invades her loving hands
of pure light, weave and coax
there way of purity

Oh Señor, master of pure love
Be with the Self of I
I am the Self, I am pure love.

Unity

She struggles to find unity;
All her life she wandered by herself,
decisions made on Inner Boundaries,
being one no more is a challenging state

How to proceed dictates her mental state,
she is mad – turmoils of truth,
but there is only one; she meditates,
she reflects on Unity, Divine Love

Reflections

Running away, moving as one
Flying high as an eagle was
Beauty, flowing low
in Truth recounts the path,

stepping stones of light
following another's path,
making footprints of time
with inner work,
looking, knowing, understanding,
compassion, humanising qualities of life.

Instinctual Self of animal
from within heart she beats
vibrations of all Mother,
Nature's tools of Self,
of Self beyond Self, of Unity of Belief.

Belief

She believes, she remembers
the essence of being,
how close to light she comes
disconnected from soul
the light shows the way, simple
buttons of flow direct
the knowledge of the thought
that forms the way to freedom of Self
that which I am, the everything.

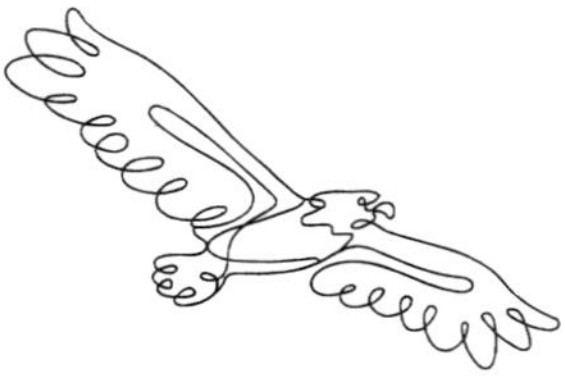

Means

What means will I use to find my way
to that where I want to be
Do I yet know where this is, this place of
Being that longs for the Soul of me

Mother Love

Light of Light sweet remembrance
Calls, to first light of Birth
Exquisite holding of embrace
Held firmly to chest of beating Heart.
I know that rhythm,
I know that sweet tone of crooning
As I am held to my Mother's sweet breast
I am held in loving arms of embrace
as eyes of love and joy and contentment gaze into mine
I am soothed, I am loved by my Mother's first touch.

Eagle Eye

From crevasses high she glides
through air of lightness,
feeling the natural wind of warmth

Over forests of green and boulders of streams
where floats the conscious mind
of madness, beneath the surface
of the flowing stream.

She banks
and with a twinkle to her eye she
submits to light unconscious
gliding through mind space
of non existence.

Waters Edge

The energy of her finds solace
At the waters edge, gently
feet that are in shallows
move to its rhythmic face,
knees sway as the energy feels
the light force of Nature's touch on bodily form
Is this the love force of humbleness, so entwined
In Nature's embrace.

Wings

Her wings flutter gently in
morning light, glistening within
deep shades of Blue, folding
unfolding as the mood dictates
warmth of Sun and Light
she dœs embrace

In Stillness He Sits

In the calmness of life
where eagles dare
silently he sits watching time move

Cascading, the water falls gently
on the rocky banks
tinkling, tinkling are the sounds that
encompass his Being

Under a tree, racing racing
he brings all of life
along with his bounding energy

Notice the stillness, Notice the gifts
Notice the twinkle of the eyes
embracing the joys of movement

In stillness he sits
quietness in the calmness
of life, he is one
with the Mother of the Earth.

Within The Light

Calm within influences the depth
Diving deep she plays within the light.
Fingers of Love gently moving,
encouraging the shyness to disappear, the
light within unfolds as the Song of Guidance
calls forth by gentle touch

Within the light all her unity of love resides

She Sings

She sings her song of silence
in a Forest of Life, where nature
calls to all its inhabitants.
I am here, I am Self
I am everything, I am silence within,
Sing my Song of Silence, be at peace

Moving Legs

Hesitantly I watch her move
across my mat, legs long
stretching to find her way
My heart beat dœs not change, my calmness remains
She moves so elegantly, Nature of Love

I Am Divine

Shall I call myself Divine
Do I know what it means
Words written on a candle holder
Catch my wandering thoughts.

To be born again I choose
Divine partnership with Life,
She is within my ever presence of being.

Divine Love, Divine Light
Divine Feminine, all are parts of my Soul
Connection with all that I am, with
all that I now want to be,
I am Divine, I am born

Mother's Embrace

My thoughts flow like the eternal stream
Encompassing all of the movement of life,
I float supported by the movement of forgetfulness
Dropping each thought as it manifests to doing.

Doing nothing, opening to all inner sensations
of non-movement, muscles let go as inner body moves,
I acknowledge I am here, I am part of the stream,
I float enwrapped in my Mother's embrace.
I float

Dripping, dripping, dripping, my footprints
move across the boulders to the flat rock of warm embrace
Spreading my naked skin against her hardness, the ever present
warmth of being here; here in my Mother's secure embrace allows
form of movement to take place. All thoughts disappear into the
warming flow of nothingness. I have arrived, I am here,
I am floating in Nature's Love, I dive deep
I float on the air of being
I float, I breathe, I awake.

Awakening Forest Of Light

In forest deep to early cock crow
the sound diminish the din of sounds alive
Like a clock of alarm she awakens
the death-like slumber of shadows of night.

In evening sun she quietens, gentle breezes flowing
through soft barriers of air – I am awake, I am here,
I am in the master's pure light, the love of light awakens
and sleep arises and diminishes as the flow
of a stream in forest's boulders

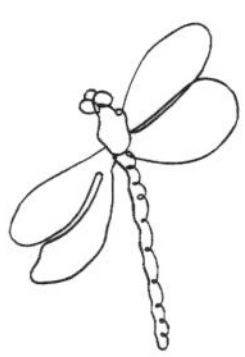

My Son Journeys Forth

Standing tall you hug me
One last time, tightening arms of encouragement
Feel life's force move, letting go, true Mother's embrace

Oh my Son, so much joy
Love, life, laughter, tears,
Words retracted after cold day,
Day deliberations have we exchanged
from time of growth for both of us.

Go discover your Soul's path, its journey of you,
Where the origin of brightness encompasses all
Live, be true, for truth to all you now hold dear
opens the chapters of the adventurous you.

The Emptying Nest

Generations of inner turmoil
Surface beyond control,
Idleness of non doing creates
A title for itself

Function, be strong, stand
Within your love, but how
When the heart of being
Is moving elsewhere, the nest
Is emptying, splintering beyond.

Letting Go

I went, he went, we all went
But who were the ones letting go
I weep at the emptiness of arms
Such freedom.

Mother's Love

They called it mother love
The snail catches up
The mushroom unfolds
The darkness receives the light

The intertwinement of the dance
Sparks many movements,
Interactions of love unfold
As understanding dawns

The Light of sunrise's beauty
Rises high over the island
Of non-observation
Dawning of loves movement ejects
An Awe from lips sealed
By the nature of childhood's passing

I am now of adulthood, expression
of Being true to me! My truth of being
embraces the joy of living and laughter of Mother's Love

Places Of Being

There are places of being
where love unfolds
Mountain falls of coolest streams
resurrect life's love for all being

The curtain of Mountains
offers passageways of cliffs
where falls so deep, cold embraces
the warmth of being

Dragonflies land, and flies of life co-exist
as the beauty of this place of being, drops
become mountain falls

sunken below, the stream of cold offers
sanctuary to those that need to heal
Coolness sometimes required to balance
the fire of life's embrace

Rock Paper Scissors

Choices against each other
Who will come true
Laughter brings all
To conclusion

Contemplation

Half in, half out, who will jump
back to back under the
Tree of Life

Splash, a gasp of air enters
the joy, breathe deeply oh
one of being

What is this movement
running towards the embrace
of the heart, music overlaps
all regrets of what it could have been
with life's passing I embraced

Depth

Where man lives in Darkness
The depth is cold and solid
A wall that light penetrates
Lifts a veil on godliness personified

Oh Darkness of Light, I am at your table of joy
and laughter, feasting on the Mother Love
of being, just here

The crickets become the orchestra of sound
Movements of cello and flute, from low to high
Pitching the echos of the music into bliss

I sit beneath the tree of contemplation
watery eyes of remote being, wash away the
struggles of penetration – I am alive with light of warmth

I rise above the cold, I float on the clearest of light
For light is all it is, this joy of life and lighter of the being of me!

The Lighthouse

I stand tall and strong
Open to all forces of
light and nature

the strength of being comes
from within, travelling far
on the boat cruise of life,
through oceans of sound

Your light draws me, its
colour ever changing, flashing
a token of music towards
those that listen

Listen, Listen, do you recognise the call
of the lighthouse, where strength of standing
lights through the ages, as tall men weep at
her light's embrace.

Breathe

The sound lingers, everlasting
It seems between gasps of life grace
Short, long, the magnitude of
the breathe escapes not a wheeze

The rattle of throat is not paramount
Life still flows through the gulp of open throat
As chest rises to meet the rhythm of movement

1,2,3,4, simple steps of counting
Rhythm, no difference between each gasp
Until slowness of rhythm introduces 5
which lingers upon exit.

The impertinence of breath to the
Rhythm of life, its warmth,
external binds do break, as its
ceasing becomes nothing

Through Time Of Love

Wrapped in arms that tighten
As upset of movement dictates
The arms of the Mother try to
Let go, but daughter does embrace

A babe in arms, snuggled deep
In fold of loves warmth embrace
Reluctant to leave the nest of
Mother loves true embrace

Statues stand in the ocean of waves,
Son of light brings warmth of heat divine
I am bereft

For now I stand alone
On morning sand, becoming a
Statue to the witness of
Life's movement through time of love

The Strength Of Love

Gently, gently, the light dances
Behind the veils of unknown words
Listening to the soft melody of Song
Language has no barriers to
The Flame of God

Oh so softly do I you embrace
For gentleness is the strength of being
To be still, to be within, to connect
With the light of love, strength unknown

Sadness erupts, through veils that lift
From thine face, behold the Mother love
Is gone, Its disappearance marks
The movement into unknown voids

Oh Mother, where thou art I cannot follow,
All I can do is feel into my being
Where the sadness and joy of the light
Of love dwells in my strongly beating heart

Language Of Light

Language of expressive tenderness
Hides behind the walls built from youth.
How do you break down the imagery of height

Access is open to all that can
See the path of light
Tenderness opens the pathways
Illumination becomes all

Shifting, shifting the light as it plays
The part of surrendered innocence
Oh the pain of such great sorrow
Opens the door to being one

Show me how she cries, in answering truth,
Light manifests, changing all on contact
Flowing between, shifting all that stands still

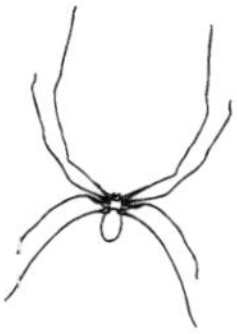

This Is Me

Beauty, this is me
To be seen takes courage of love
Unfolding petals gently moving
On the breeze

To be seen, to allow oneself the
Pleasure of being, how much love
can one hold, I am seen,
I put myself in the arms of God

Trauma of living, oh so separate
from the beings of love, that
gently move within. Oh my God,
your breeze ignites the longing

Where are you now as I sit within
Can I see you
My heart beats the drum of life
I am seen, this is me, my beauty unfolds.

Brushing One's Path

She gently sweeps the path
Oh the beauty of youth
So much to learn

Ants continue to crawl, their path,
Under the sweeping brush it lies
So dedicated to being, she sweeps
The path of life

Beneath the trees the chattering
Chicos and chicas exchange words
of meaning, eating on the fruits of
Labour, shadow and sunshine integrates all

One sits alone, peaceful in memories
Of being, quietness she dœs not know
But slowly oh so slowly she sweeps
Clean the chatter of life

Boxes Of The Mind

How many boxes can we hold
One for this, one for that
Placing them carefully within the
Circular mind.

Like a sack where do we put them
To create the canvas of non-thought
Separation to the corners of the mind

The canvas of being is here and now
Where all thought manifests, blank as the boxes
One filled to be brought slowly to the table

The inspection of being, acceptance of all,
loving all that opens shadow and shade, light and dark
they are all metaphors of love, the pain and the joy

The Gentleness Of Love

The gentleness of love,
hiding deeply within
So beautiful to see everyday
The longing is so painful to see, face
Just the way you are

Beauty hidden deep, to embrace the content
Of being who you are- music of life, connections
Of source, the soul dances with light

Laughter of life, the joy of living
Allows the gentleness to love unfold
From deep within the body of life

I am gentle, as a breeze on a hot summer's day
That touches the skin of self
Softly opening the pores where
Darkness has lain, cleansing the
Being of light

Vibration Of Love

Gently welcoming vibration of love
Closeness of a hug with arms embrace
Vibration of love, offering the nurture of Soul

Singing, Nature of Sound, quietness prevails
The chatter of human tone – all encompassing
Vibration of heart, welcome the light of love

Stretching the muscle tone,
Strength to endure the vibration of the
Awakening paths of light
The body ignites the Soul of living

The being remembers the vibration of love
Through hidden veils its connection prevails
Where art thou oh father of love
The light in the light, my daughter vibrates

Simple Beauty

What is simple? To clean repetitively,
to sweep continuous, to obey the Master,
Oh heart of hearts, so simple it seems to be beautiful

The connection of beauty, of sunlight, of gentleness
Oh so soft light of beauty, where do you shine
on Living Soul.

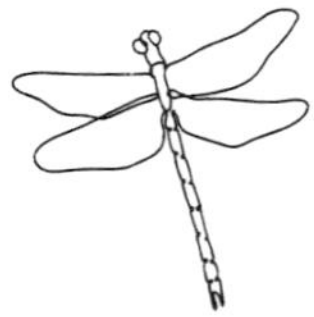

The kiss, the hug, the beauty of love
Expression comes naturally to all that
dwell in the casa of simplicity.
Beauty beholds all that enter her gates

In the order, the order of being
Where perfection lies, it's simple -
Beauty that projects the order of time

But the choices of love also injects
The purity of living, of discovering of faith
The beauty of the nurturing of the soul to expansion
Simple beauty of growth into Le Luv (the light)

The Fruit

Bursting forth is sweet caress
The taste is dramatic, awakening unfolds
Not just fruit but all that came before
Its growth brings the taste of Mother alive

Juices flow across the tongue
Oh how imagined they caress the
Taste buds of life, their light brings
Forth the memory of growth

All the influences brought forth
That connect their origin of being
Become part of the transmission of
Their sweet caress
Oh fruit of love, I gorge on
Thy tender softness of heart
Where infinite chambers connect
Thou sweetness of being

Vibration Of Loving Sound

The being of Self eternal love
Internalises the vibration of being
Being with the Soul of expansion within

Softly softly like a child peeping out behind a door
Love beckons gently encouraging her steps
Of movement.

Attunment To The Heart

Little by little she let her go
To ancestor of light
Her place prepared, Mother & Daughter reunite

Stepping into life she is now found
Hiding no longer in the majesty of
The outdoor, life now becomes her

Embracing love energy
Vitality, freedom, love, prosperity, abundance
The blockages are gone, all are now her entwined

Oh Guardian Angel I do love you so,
Angel of sisterhood, I let you go.
Tears of joy are now the shedding force of love

Loss Of Time

At a time of great loss
At a time of great worry
There is a time to move
And a time to stay,
What is time but that of being

Heavens of madness encompass
My brain, what have I loosened
upon this earth.
Within the forces speak
what are they but signatures through time

The earth moves on her axis of strength,
Like a merry go 'round of space in time
Her sister sun hides and peeps out from
Horizons of light - glorious effigies
Of time's embrace, the decay of
Movement in time

Come to me, come to me, vibrate your
Inner peace, the gentleness of all knowing, the eternal
Light of grace, the Master holds the aura of light

Opening, opening to the light, the path of
Consciousness unfolds, the light, the path, the beauty
Beckons as the child steps forth to womanhood embrace
Vibrating the Sound of Love

The Gentleness Of Soul

In the gentleness of our soul we find ourselves
We may be high on adrenalin
Of fear, anxiety, overwhelm
All states of being that we are

Come my friends feel the flow of love
Love of self, love of being, love of this new way
Engage with who you are, engage with the Self
For love of being unites us all.

Embrace the tree of life, the energy & strength of being
Being one, being of one, seeing the branches
Feeling the silence of the sap that unites us all

We are the tree of life, together we are a gentleness of soul
Connecting to source
We find ourselves our flow, our love, our being

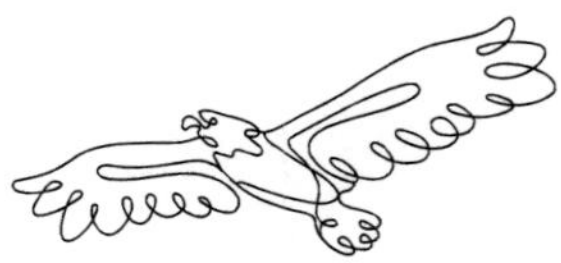

About The Author

Energy healer, educator and avid surfer Linda Barry Tuohy's path has never veered too far from sea and soul. Serving in cliff rescue and RLNI in the 1980's, Linda founded Oceanics Surf School in 1997, which was then the only school of its kind in Ireland. Linda led and pioneered activities encouraging women into the sport of surfing and entrepreneurial enterprises incorporating lifestyle living.

After immersing herself in meditation, she moved into the world of mystic healing. Learning to transmit loving energy, Linda founded LBT (LoveBeingTrue) her multi dimensional and Applied biomagnetic therapy practice in 2015.

Connecting to Source - A path to self-discover through verse is her first collection, and is a continuation of her own journey towards self-realisation, self-discovery and the process of reconnecting with the Mother Love, the unconscious and the Divine.

Linda is married to Paul, and they have two adult children, Jai & Raya. She divides her time between Tramore in Co Waterford Ireland, and Mallorca in the Balearic Islands.